My Bodies This Morning This Evening

Eve Esfandiari-Denney is a poet of mixed heritage from South London. Her writing centers on reflexive interrogations of the categories that constitute selfhood; nationhood, citizenship, gender and the material body. She is currently the Birch Family scholar studying an MA in Creative Writing at UEA following her BA at Goldsmiths University.

GW00683444

My Bodies This Morning This Evening

Published by Bad Betty Press in 2022
www.badbettypress.com

Cover illustration by Nina Carter

Printed and bound in the United Kingdom

A CIP record of this book is available from the British Library.

ISBN: 978-1-913268-24-4

Supported using public funding by
ARTS COUNCIL ENGLAND

LOTTERY FUNDED

My Bodies
This Morning
This Evening

For Helen & Robbie

*Thank you for your unobligated and infinite support,
for leaving your front door on the latch.*

PRESS

the ultimate claustrophobia is the syllogism
the ultimate claustrophobia is "it all adds up"

– Diane di Prima, *Rant*, 1985

Contents

Sunbird doubting

I want to be in daylight without a witness,
                  separate myself from the doer,
                  be near water.

I mumble when I fly, it's weird.

Did I miss the turning into the sun
when asking for miracles; a job.

        When I tried on love like a wetsuit
and broke into a golf course

                          pouring down
silver on lawns
in winter until I was bird now.

Love's Valley kept ruined by stains, oh floral blood!

I want you to hold my hand,

use your other hand to hold a falcon on my behalf.

I can explain; the shore is covered in shuddering fish for a reason—

it's your fog horn,
how you prioritise work in the morning.

Look, I covered my entire body in arnica for you;
love isn't logic.

It's a beautiful tile,
like piercing a song with a pin and letting the life out, it's to sleep
alone but so wild with new atoms.

Good and better lies

          like this, wearing a veil I will evade evil on my way
up the escalator while on the phone to my sisters.
When exile began, I turned my head to laugh. I chose one stem
of thyme, a handful of barberry, a spoon of burnt sugar.
The market floor is the basics of theatre. From Isfahan

to beyond river Karkheh, meaning Four Edens, meaning
you can find a canoe between borders
of paradise. When all allocated segments

of holy and half holy water were behind me
I ignored my city; ignored my rain; ignored my nosebleed.
Don't worry, the way to begin in another place is about arriving.

Soraya, Damsa, Shirin, here I have told them we drink,
I have told them we dance, I have tried violet creams,
lemon meringue pie from England.

I was promised I could cut clean hair in salons and play
the quiet war in our house from a radio like a song
our mother is crying in.

I have forgotten homesickness is a bridal hormone,
that some of us claim there is a city near the sun
liberated by a commander woman and if you die
by the hand of a daughter you will not go to paradise. Tonight

I am craving liver and earth, you sisters.
I have more in common with the properties
of birdsong than this language:

A proud cuckoo will mimic the orientation of the satellites,
the public silence between sun keepers,
the plural voice of the commander
when she said   *annunciate   you have permission to sing.*

No one knows who my Grandfather is, not Aunty Queenie, Uncles Motshan, Ocean or Vano

Hey stranger   your replica is my father
his face like an altar of your objects
a gathering of small white stones   the shape of teeth
a bowl or a mortar for a skull.   Each mineral iris
is what is made lifelike   like a father
or water   every eye moves along a bloodline
a galleried helix   lighting up   each
bright   dead   brown   *yok* is *eye*
is a moving place
the way a spirit falls and is glass-blown into a sphere.
Earthing a portrait of a man who spat a sun-flower seed
loosened his belt   my Grandfather or shadow-puppet
pressed into the arched bones of my family nose
translating a foot   leaving Gobi sand
a foot a foot a foot a daffodil   pronounced *dyker*
like a disturbance to the ecosystem
a long line of caravans depart   blur into shells self-shushing.

The Roma word

for ***moon***   is   ***shon*** like past-tense shining,
can you hear the way Dharamshala echoes
unfolding its letters after transit. For Romani
"naak" is (nose)-*naak*, **"munh"** is (mouth)-*munh*.

Solo to bird phoenix

After Attar'

      I know you can see through my body,
its soft little bones
its heart-shrill rhythm.
I forget how astral everything is, that my suffering

is equivocal to my orchard, the number of orange fruits that exist.

      I love the way your beak is pierced with exactly a thousand holes.
      Each opening has a different sound, each sound is a secret.

Phoenix, I tried to rip the skin off a snake instead of letting it moult.
I tried to block sunlight with my body, save a fly from a swimming pool.

I've tried to live my life in one breath,
tried rebirth, trusted I am a butterfly
dreaming as a woman; the fact there are realised beings.

Don't tell Oaba, Baba-joon
about my drinking
rainwater through dirt.

About my opening the door to death like a boathouse.
That I am only blood mixed with dust and dust
and the world might persuade you otherwise.

vultures are singing

Hello,   will you cry your heart out
when I address you;   Commissioner Seahorse, Delegate Butter
Angel   Speaker Warm Water
Council of all gentle things.

I am seventeen and dying of cancer   today
someone read my body back. Its blood type,   the atomic weight
the   number   of   bones;   I don't trust any of them
so contingent on   each other, on   gentle things.

Council, it hurts when you   lead me in by   my carpet burns,
by my ankles.   Even during   slow moving
traffic,   this fruit drink   you could let me
leave. I imagine I can go anywhere   to fiber-optic cables
or submarine cables   at any moment I could cross
the Atlantic. I am already leaving moving like   landscapes   do

so elastic, like   how there is a place to tread
between   hell and   the light from the fridge or,
how there are so many sim cards beneath the Ozone.   They are
hidden everywhere, the same as ants.   To you,

I hold up one big hand   then one little hand   as if surrender
can be had.   I'm asking you   Agent
Milkweed,   understudy to   Seahorse,
formerly known as   Rain Bird, all gentle.

Would you   make me   fight   there is more
to life than more   of it.   To conserve is   to imagine
permanence as if   we could not revert back to what we were
before,   we could not
be proteins. Let me   trade

a light for my home   when my powered down
body   is entire   in the bath   after dinner, it's
tired it can't keep tiring.   You know the reason a bird sings
in the morning is to confirm she survived the night you know
to survive   is to gather what you have until something
changes   my alkalines,   my blindfold beyond medicine,

the familiar lilt in a voice moving closer; all   gentle things
                                        turn
around.   I had you   I'll undo myself to see you later.

~ This Is Medium World 7 ~

Myself and then my body are
sipping sequin-coloured Oxy through
a vein on the edge of light.
In my nightgown i levitate
from the Oncology unit
to the nearby bar, *Genuine Liquorette*.
There, a swan drifts past
behind me at the pace of a funeral
and i ask the bouncer

> *What's that absolute*
classic Ibiza tune; dun dun dundun
you know..
He says:
> *Darude, Sandstorm.*
and what did i come here for again, oh yeah,
i'm in Medium World 7
feat. the horses from the Lloyds TSB advert
running *running!* with me along a five-mile
prayer mat towards the smoking area and

> i can't keep my mouth closed.
i ask a stranger:
How do you keep your mouth closed?
But we are in Medium World 7,
possession is not like protection there is only
the distance between an amoeba and a lake.

So i'm swaying…
or walking,   bypassing Papa Smurf and
what a mess in me my glass
floods with ice as the sky opens
and the ambulance arrives. A paramedic
takes me by the hand back
into the tubular where
Medium World 7 will stop moving on

          and on its axis.
i was so sad when they folded me back
into the sheets of the portable bed returning
to a room dying could enter.

For Patty and Selma

For Cress and me

there will always be yearning & worship in the company of another
booming heart crying like a mammal over soap stars.

Your life are one painful, beautiful pregnancy. Alone in your carpeted
bungalow heaving ropes of air you chain-smoke in bed,
tell apart each of your breasts like four cow bells in violet wire-bras.

~ O Patty, count the objects in the room & sip a White Russian, Selma. ~

Your boneless yellow body & fatty hearts
adhere to what is difficult. What it means
to "yield half smashed-up things and call it commonality".
Patty said *Patty, I mean Selma*
        I could switch off the TV set & sit here in the dark with you forever.

in this rented loft conversion

there is a space to cram the sky
and i am so surprised you cycled here when you are tired
like this above the night gem
slow-moving lorries
at 10:00pm we leave to buy a carton of grape

and walking along the flat road
you point to komodos
in adverts
and the florescence humming
in corners of bus stop screens in rows
and rows
and i realise incidentally you are left handed too
it has been a year of not knowing
this about you or much else

i've been leaning into caution
all this time so sedate with beer at night
i'm nervous but what kind of moon will hear
about it besides
i should have known
from things like a bad song called feelings
or my high breath in
from when you wash your body
i have watched you so often

a chest full pour of water
over all of you
everywhere in the bath with you at night
i hear the birds outside move in one miraculous lift.

As for seeing you

      I'll need to learn English again
and ring all these holy bells.
Here is a very sexy picture
of Mary, bleeding.
      Leyly, I saw you at the party and a second body fell out of me.
It had a face as sunny as a nut. A stomach full of bambiness
and bulbs its legs two hairy angels puckering lip balm
and striding towards you to then only
carry me home, awkwardly, tenderly.

I do not shadowbox myself, loosen my yeeha! And gallop on

Have you noticed
I am often longing into beads
pressing my face into walls
when you leave

I wait for you in bathwater
I do not drink the bathwater.
All that's left here
is my grown-up body
it is what it is   particle

by particle   vacating
in sediments and moving
away in silent confetti

you are loved and are capable of love
and dissolving and reforming
in a cluster of light,   again I do
what I like, I suppose.

I prepare my interior
by warming the air, ensuring
I am a well-lit place
for *god to enter my body*
as a body my same size.

After Leyly

O my ovarian health! the beat of ah! the white of your eyes,
the white of your eyes so like glass-bottled milk your mouth
so mouth i do drunken love i do i do lay down my lights
beside a plate of tomatoes

you grated *thank you*; i want to laugh like you now,
prove to everyone that has loved you they were right
every night-walking Juliette every girl Saint
Flora clean from the body

they will hold you up one by one with one
hundred found strong arms like we all should have. Please wait,

let me store your breaths in sound fields so I can play them back,
then play them again in reverse until morning, morning lay down
your lights like a sun controlling a world again what a well

choreographed thing you you bending the tendons
of my knees so my thighs are against my chest are against
my ah's my every my every bright bone will
break   by tenderness   here is a party made out of almost no one.

Just rice and string, the smell of your room, your body in shorts,
a big goose in my chest
          my goose my goose my goose my goose

will you find a way to get into the ground so you can hear
a ring sound glowing; lean too far forward into its heat
straining to say and then saying *i do*

not hope for a fresh water fountain; a new white saint bird;
a deep down down animal. i don't want any of it i don't
want the name someone else will give me.

She will call me water but i will be moving an ore
an ore in water Leyly Leyly *there is no such thing as repetition.*
Only insistence i wake up tomorrow without you without
you there sleeping and say it again.

I am a big baby girl

I bump bellies with a bloat of sadness   link my thumbs and spread my hands
to flap them

up

and down,

up

like wings slow to the sound of ambient pipe music
falling on loop.
                This is a remedy I recommend to you after the death of your mother.

It will sooth a hard nut in the throat, one that shines   speaks
to people about its hardness.
                    The maternal parts of your hips will be obvious after.
                        Bear down on these bones while you dress yourself
in various shades of gingham.   Squat wide and breach good
            always in dresses piss   on nights out between cars.
Hold your chubby hands together and Push!
                                            Push!
the urgent waters for a life bathed in lamp-light to appear.
It won't and it's true, I cry about it, I am a bad mother.
                I try to fantasize about speaking like mothers should.
                        Today would be a chat about the virtues;
the chicken carcass, the black hair dye, the everything ticking on.

But when I'm upset I do drive myself to the maternity ward;
I show them my sex and ask them what it is.

They confirm I am a baby girl, a big baby girl. I am lovely
my body O! its heavy falling and nightly crying,
its blue sweet tongue, *listen listen* what I know I don't understand.

As for the love of beautiful creatures

       I believe in a bag of wet bikinis,
the tradition of sadness,
that everywhere is a mother dying
as a mother does forever mutilated

and sleeping, spinning light and organs like ribbons
leaving the TV screen. I told my mother *let them*

push the needle in. That armada
of cancers inside her, building one more
hard yellow mountain. I hoped every 4am

a Hoopoe bird would land on her body,
its wings could slap
the skin of her chest to give rhythm;

Where is

hope beyond the cabbage patch,   *where are you going.*

All the while the new season is turning its dirt,
Spring has begun, and to think
I had once been live in her belly, a sack of organs

inside one of hers. Just like a girl on a stretcher
you could have considered me a civilian
when they found me blood-bodied, panting

rolling around on my back
exposing my stomach in submission. My

Mother. I dug out these daffodils
with my mouth for her
during those Aprils which I trusted
would not end her life until I made it back.

She was meant to see these petals unharden
to bloom like a bomb;
here is the sound of Spring going silent.

Notes

The poem "Sunbird doubting" responds to Farīd-od-Dīn Attar'
translated text: *The Canticle of the Birds*, in particular the poem "The
birds ask the Hoope to resolve their doubts". "Love's Valley kept
ruined by stains, oh floral blood!" also draws directly on the same
text by referencing one of the Seven Valleys; the Valley of Love,
where reason is abandoned for the sake of love.

"Solo to bird phoenix" considers the Simurgh, a mythical bird
prevalent in the writing of Farīd-od-Dīn Attar'.

"~ This Is Medium World 7 ~" paraphrases an Angel Nafis line:
"show me a room dying can't enter" in her poem "Ghazal to Open
Cages".

In "For Patty and Selma": "your life are one painful beautiful
pregnancy" and "yield half smashed up things and call it
commonalty" are a paraphrase and quotation from Rainer Rilke's
Letters to a Young Poet.

"in this rented loft conversion" ends on a phrase indebted to a line
in Joe Carrick-Varty's poem, "Lop Nur" which reads "the birds
inexplicably lifting".

"As for seeing you" includes lines from Anne Sexton poem "Flee on
Your Donkey" when her poem reads "two hairy angles" and "carry
me home, awkwardly, tenderly".

"After Leyly" paraphrases "there can be no repetition because the
essence of that expression is insistence" from Gertrude Stein's
"Portraits and repetition".

"I am a big baby girl" adapts a line from Kaveh Akbar's poem "Vines": "I am lovely too my body".

"I do not shadowbox myself, loosen my yeeha! And gallop on" quotes "God entered my body as a body my same size"- Unknown, from a Craigslist listing for a used 2001 Ford Escape.

"As for the love of beautiful creatures" is heavily inspired by the meditations on Spring in Derek Jarman's film *Last of England*, 1987.

Acknowledgements

Many thanks to *bath magg*, *The Manchester Review*, *Polyester zine*, *Riggwelter Press* and The White Review Poet's Prize for publishing early versions of these poems. Thank you to Devotion, Faber Academy, Goldsmiths University, Royal Holloway and UEA for your scholarships that have collectively offered me an invaluable education in literature.

My sincerest thanks to all my teachers, friends, family and Bad Betty Press. In particular my Dad, Rachael Allen, Joe Carrick-Varty, Joe Hunt, Lara Laeverenz, Daljit Nagra, Gboyega Odubanjo, Hannah Taverner, Jack Underwood and Memoona Zahid who have offered their encouragement or/and editorial efforts for the making of this collection.

Lightning Source UK Ltd.
Milton Keynes UK
UKHW010007130922
408733UK00001B/254

9 781913 268244